HOW TO LIVE

Peter Johns

London | New York

Contents

First Words

I wrote and self-published this book for my daughter, Meg, and gave it to her as a present on her eighteenth birthday. As a birthday present it would almost certainly have been close to the bottom of her wish list, but I had a particular reason for doing so.

For most young people this time of life is a particularly stressful one and in many ways Meg is an ordinary girl. But in one way she is unusual because, when she was younger, she was diagnosed with cancer. I was already aware that, as many studies have shown, the long-term issues associated with anxiety and depression for survivors of childhood cancers are higher than for the population at large. She was also just about to take her A Level exams and I wanted to support her in any way I could. I had had the idea of writing a book for her for some time, and I had written down some ideas, but it was only as her birthday approached that I began to do something about it.

I am not a medical person. When Meg's doctor first told me the name of the cancer that had attacked her it had seemed so strange and remote from the real world it was something I could barely

1

comprehend. But I came to know the name well in the long months of treatment that followed and I shall never forget it. She had a T-cell lymphoblastic lymphoma and she was only nine years old.

Meg's lymphoma took the form of a rapidly developing tumour that had grown within her chest cavity and, by the time of its diagnosis, was already so large that it was beginning to crush her lungs. The initial diagnosis as an outpatient was relatively optimistic. I was told that she did have a tumour but that it was obviously benign because, given its size, if it had been malignant she would certainly be dead. The diagnosis was wrong: the tumour was malignant in every way it is possible to be. When we got her to hospital the following day her lungs had started to collapse and she spent many days under sedation, attached to a machine that did her breathing for her.

When she was well enough she began chemotherapy. After four months the tumour was reduced in size, but to our dismay a second tumour had started to grow. This development, known as a 'progression', was at that time regarded as fatal and we were told as much. Fortunately, with the help of an inspired doctor, a perfect bone marrow match with one of her brothers, and many sessions of total body irradiation, she survived.

As Meg grew towards adulthood and her anxieties about life in general appeared to be increasing, I began to think about how I had felt at a similar age. Although I never had to experience what Meg went through, my own early days had not been without stress and anxiety and they were certainly without success. So I thought I might have something useful to tell her about how, when life seems low, it will pass; when it's hard see a way forward, it will resolve; and that trying to make the most of whatever life offers is the best way to live. There is nothing new or profound in these sentiments, but in the book I tried to present them in a way that made them relevant to her, and to me.

How to Live is therefore a book about simple strategies that I wrote down for my daughter in an effort to help her through life, and my hope is that what I have written may also have sufficient resonance with other readers to help them too. But in a deeper sense the title is for Meg. When the second tumour was confirmed, and hope for her survival was hanging by a thread, the words for us, her parents, were not a topic but a question that we

---

asked ourselves in some desperation on her behalf:
How to Live?

I wrote the book in six weeks and a dozen copies
arrived with a week to spare before her eighteenth
birthday. Apart from some minor changes and a
small number of additions including these First
Words, this is the book I gave her.

Peter Johns

Prologue –
A Rite of Passage

For thousands of years, humans have marked the transition from child to adult by subjecting initiates to rites of passage. These ceremonies were often brutal and involved ritual humiliation, violent beatings, tests of endurance, physical mutilation of the most awful kind and long periods of solitary seclusion away from the rest of the tribe. Similar ceremonies still exist in some tribal societies and there the first steps to becoming an adult can be a terrifying and painful experience.

Today you are eighteen and it's time for your own rite of passage. Fortunately this is Britain in the twenty-first century and we've made some progress; now all that happens is you get a book from your Dad.

PART ONE

ABOUT THIS BOOK

Setting the Scene

This little book is a small collection of thoughts and reflections that have helped me through my own life and which seemed to me to be worth writing down. It's intended to be a book that you can read straight through, turn to a specific topic, or dip into at random when you have a free minute or two.

Despite the book's title you will not find much in it about morals, nor about how to behave. I am not saying that morals are not important, just that you must make your own decisions on those issues. Morals are no more than a set of guidelines for treating others with fairness and respect. Some people claim they tell us something more profound about good and evil, but I don't accept that. What I do believe is that people are born with an innate sense of right and wrong, and of what is fair and what is not. Unless that innate sense has been corrupted by genes or by upbringing most people understand the difference.

Rather than a moral guide, the book is – or at least tries to be – a manual for living. In that sense it is similar to a manual for operating a washing machine. That manual won't tell you how to build a new washing machine, but it will perhaps help you to get the best from the one you already have.

I've thought about most of the subjects in this book for many years. In my early life I had some difficult times and perhaps they would have been resolved sooner if I had known then what I know now.

But I've still had a lot of fun in my life. One day it will come to an end, as it does for all of us, but while I have a working body and a mind that functions I will go on enjoying life as well as I can. I hope you will too, and I hope that what follows will help.

A Fulfilled Life

Simply put, this book is about how to live your life in such a way that it makes you happy to be living it. That is what I call a fulfilled life. To be more specific is not possible because, although there are some common themes, there are as many ways of living a fulfilled life as there are people on the planet. In Britain such a life might include at least some of the following: a measure of success, the respect of others, an inquisitive mind, a few close friends and perhaps a settled home life.

In other less stable parts of the world we might add water, food and sanitation to the list of requirements and probably place the emphasis on those three. The point is there is no absolute measure. Fulfilment is possible wherever we can find it.

There is though one important theme common to all fulfilled lives, which is an interest in activities that, in themselves, are not essential to the business of living. Arts, hobbies, sport and leisure all fall into this category but there are many others. Why humans should not simply be machines for living is not clear, but we are not. We are more, and need something more from life. That 'something' is one of the subjects of this book.

In countries like Britain there is an emphasis on success, which is measured in many forms: wealth, achievement and celebrity are three examples. I have had some success in my career and many friends have too. All of us have been lucky as well as working hard, although not all would admit it. But wealth, achievement or celebrity on their own don't seem to be sufficient to achieve a life that can be called fulfilled. That comes more from living your life as well as you can and achieving, or striving for, excellence in all that you do. Sometimes your efforts to achieve excellence will bring you wealth, achievement or celebrity, but it is the striving for excellence rather than the result that contributes most towards fulfilment.

There is something more than that too. Whatever wealth, achievements and fame you gather in your life, it is the feeling that you are living a just life, a life where what you have has been earned and where you enjoy the respect of those you love, those are the things that mean the most.

This book will not provide you with a road map to fulfilment but it will try to point you in the right direction. The journey itself you have to make on your own.

PART TWO

ABOUT LIFE

Climb the Mountain

I use an analogy that compares life to climbing a mountain. Life involves a similar climb except that you can never get to the summit. Sometimes the path seems easy and you have time to admire the view, like when you pass your exams with top grades, or you fall in love with someone who loves you too, or you get the job you've always wanted.

But sometimes you come to a part of the mountain where the cliff overhangs and the mist comes down; you can't see where to put your hands, your feet scramble for purchase and you feel afraid and scared that you might fall. Then you have to use courage and determination to keep climbing. Sometimes it can be tough and often you want to quit. But whatever happens, whether walking along the gentler slopes or attempting to scale steep cliffs and rocky overhangs, never stop trying to reach the top of the mountain, even though you know you never will.

This book will help you to make that climb. It starts with Three Rules that you have to learn, because they are all necessary for achieving fulfilment. And I don't mean just learning the words; you will have to learn how to make each of the Three Rules an integral part of your life.

Rule One: Live a Full Life

The first, and perhaps most obvious, rule for living a fulfilled life is that you must live a life that is full of experiences. Although many people disagree, I am clear that everything that happens to us takes place between the date of our birth and the date of our death. There isn't anything else.

For those who think that death is not the end, and that our presence on the planet has been ordained by some non-human entity, I don't believe the argument differs much. If we have been put here for a purpose it cannot have been for us to do nothing. To live must be to experience, whether we exist by chance or by design.

To the young, life seems very long and I'm sure that for you it seems to stretch out before you as an endless journey, but for me, looking back, it doesn't seem such a long time at all. This is a normal perspective for both of us, given our respective ages, but it also shows that you too will one day look back and ask where all the years went.

So, in the small time you have available, concentrate on getting all the joy, pleasure, love and enlightenment that you can. Travel, learn, care, experience, commit as much as it is possible for you to do. Try to live your life in such a way that you don't end up with profound regrets about the opportunities you never got round to exploring, the roads you never took. You have a single opportunity, a single life. Don't waste it.

Gregory Corso, an American poet, wrote: 'Life is a century, Death an instant'. It means that life is all there is.

Rule Two: Know Who You Are

But filling your life with experiences, however enjoyable each one may be, is still not sufficient, because a life that is apparently full can still seem empty. We have all heard of people who seemed to have everything they could want but still lived their lives in despair and sometimes ended them by suicide. What went wrong?

A key step towards fulfilment is to know who you are, an idea that goes back to the Ancient Greeks. Socrates said that to know yourself you must examine your life and that: 'the unexamined life is not worth living'. He meant we have to look inside ourselves to understand the true value and meaning of our lives. We need to understand why we do what we do and think what we think. We have to list all our faults, failings and weaknesses as well as our strengths and, when doing so, be honest with ourselves and not cheat! Otherwise we are only deluding ourselves, and self-delusion makes a fulfilled life impossible to achieve.

Socrates also said that most people hold values and beliefs that are irrational or inconsistent with what they otherwise consider to be true. He said that our values and beliefs should therefore be tested regularly against what we know and, if necessary, we should modify or replace them. Only through this process of self-examination and self-renewal could we really come to 'know' ourselves.

Socrates was right to say that knowing yourself is a necessary precondition to living a fulfilled life, but I'm not sure that failure to do so, on its own, would make life 'not worth living'. I can think of many horrible things that could make your life not worth living, but a failure to examine it is not necessarily one of them.

His advice also invites a question. What if, after carefully examining your life, you still conclude it's not up to much?

Acknowledging your faults and weaknesses and understanding your many imperfections brings humility. This is a necessary condition for the achievement of a fulfilled life. Even so, without something more, it is still not enough.

Rule Three: Think Positively

So, if you are living a life full of experiences and you have carefully examined who and what you are, what's next? This third rule is about positive thinking and why some days seem to be happy and successful while others are not. It's about whether good feelings come randomly or whether you have the power yourself to determine what happens in your life and how best you can live and enjoy it.

The answer is surprising but fundamental. Life tends to live up (or down) to our expectations. That is why you should never start a day by thinking how awful it is going to be: think how good it is going to be instead. It makes it more likely that good things will happen. This is the power of positive thinking and you can try it at any time of day. Think positive thoughts before an exam, or an interview or before anything about which you are worried. Try to imagine how well you are going to perform and how good you will feel when it's over and you have passed the exam or been offered the job.

Positive thinking is also about your internal dialogue, how you talk to yourself. You must try to convince yourself that positive outcomes result from your own actions and that you are responsible for your own happiness. Most of the time this is true even if you don't actually notice it. When good things happen to you, praise yourself for making them happen and try never to assume that anything good is a lucky chance that is unlikely to occur again.

Similarly, try not to blame yourself for bad things happening; tell yourself they are the fault of external circumstances or plain bad luck. Of course, if you have done something stupid you have to own up, but most misfortunes are largely down to chance and the only effect of blaming yourself is to lower your feelings of self worth. The purpose of positive thinking is to think better of ourselves, not less, because in doing so we increase our capacity to deal more competently with life.

Positive thinking is one of the most important tools we have for directing and enhancing our lives, not just single days or single events. For some people thinking this way comes naturally but, for those to whom it doesn't, it is a technique that can be learned. Reputable studies have shown that positive thinkers are physically and mentally fitter, have higher energy levels, lower rates of depression and cope better with stress. There is even evidence that they live longer lives.

Three Rules for Living

Live a full life; know yourself; and think positively. Make these Three Rules a part of everything you do until they become as natural and familiar to you as eating or sleeping. It will take some daily effort on your part to begin with but, if you can do that, you will be surprised at how quickly your relationship with life changes for the better.

What follows in the rest of the book is, more or less, about applying the Three Rules to the business of living. But first you need to know something about life skills, the skills that people need to use every day if they are to live successful and fulfilled lives. Life skills really follow from the Three Rules and they do come naturally to some, but most people have to learn them.

Unfortunately they did not come naturally to me.

PART THREE

ABOUT ME
(AND ABOUT YOU TOO)

Life Skills

I said earlier that I had some difficult times when I was younger and from my mid-teens onwards I started behaving badly, both academically and socially. In those years I had no moral base and no guiding principles about how to live. I had become rebellious, irresponsible and unhappy in ways, and for reasons, I did not really understand.

There was nothing in my background that explains why this should have been so. My childhood was happy, in memory at least, and my parents were both good people (you knew them!). We were poor by today's standards, without electricity or running water, in a small terraced house where eight people slept in three bedrooms and I shared a bedroom, and a bed, with my grandfather. But these were conditions familiar to millions in the decade or so after World War 2, particularly in industrial South Wales where poverty was normal. We – or at least I – were unaware of any other way of living.

This lack of knowledge about other ways of living did have an important downside: it meant that our horizons and ambitions were severely restricted. I'm sure that this failure to look outwards still applies in those deprived areas that still exist in too many parts of Britain today. Being unaware of other opportunities stifles ambition, because how can people strive for advancements that they know nothing about? I remember being mesmerised by *The Forsyte Saga*, released as a BBC TV series in 1967 (when I was nineteen) and based on the books by John Galsworthy. It was the first time, even in fiction, that I had seen wealthy people interact as people. I would stop short of describing Soames Forsyte as a positive influence on my life (after all, he did rape his wife) but he certainly made me aware for the first time that there were different ways in which it was possible for people to live.

Partly for these reasons, as I approached adulthood, I needed to use life skills that might have come more naturally if I had experienced a more broadly based childhood. Life skills are simply about learning to think and behave in ways that are likely to enhance your life, rather than diminish it. It's what this book is about! In my early years I lacked such skills and I think that is why the early part of my life proved to be so difficult. I did eventually come to realise that I needed to change something, but at the time I had no idea what needed to be changed, still less what I should do to change it.

For people who lack life skills and are unaware of their importance, acquiring them can be difficult. Usually it needs some outside help.

Use Mentors

A mentor can be anyone who impresses you enough to make you want to emulate them. They are usually older than you and, if they are to be effective, they should be wiser about at least one aspect of living. Mentors don't need to know that they are your mentor and you don't need to talk to them about it, although sometimes it helps if you do. That's up to you. For my part I only ever watched, listened and reflected and, to the best of my knowledge, my mentors were never aware of the major roles that they each played in my life.

I have used mentors since my late teens (see also 'But be Realistic') but my first was by far the most important. I met Glyn Gould at a time when my life was at a very low ebb. I had dropped out of university and had found work as a croupier in the casino at the Stoneleigh Club in Porthcawl. Initially it had seemed quite glamorous. The early James Bond films had been released and I was smartly and appropriately dressed in black tie and dinner jacket. I was still to reach the age of twenty.

Glyn was an unlikely figure to inspire me. He was then sixty-one, the gaming manager at the Stoneleigh Club, responsible for the blackjack and roulette tables on which I worked. He had been a coal miner in a Welsh valley near Maesteg until a cart, used for transporting coal underground, slipped its brakes, ran down an incline and pinned him against the coal face, severing his arm just above the elbow.

Glyn was given a prosthetic arm, made of metal, and he called it Charlie. It was heavy, with a brown leather glove covering the prosthetic hand, half closed to form a kind of fist. He always joked that if there was any trouble at the Club he would hit the perpetrators with Charlie and that would be that. Such was the regard in which he was held, he never had to use it.

Glyn was transparently honest and his integrity shone from him in a way that I had not experienced before. But he was earthy and good-humoured and he never preached. Other people could do what they wanted as far as he was concerned, but for him there was only one way. He had something in common with the old Welsh non-conformist Christians, rigorous and unyielding in the way he chose to live his life but, unlike them, he was funny too. Never a religious man, his creed came from a belief that there was a right way to live and a wrong way, and he had made a conscious decision to choose the former.

On Saturday nights, after the gaming tables had closed and we had cleared up, he would invite me back to his flat with one or two of the other croupiers. There he would serve us glasses of whisky and bowls of warmed-up cawl, the Welsh broth made with vegetables and lamb. We would spend our time talking about life and the world, often past dawn.

I worked with Glyn at the Club for three years before I decided to go back to university. Initially I was intrigued by him rather than converted. But gradually I came to see that he was right; that his way of living was a good way and it was certainly better than the way that I had been living my own life. Eventually, in the fullness of time, I started trying to live my life as he had lived his. I never fully succeeded of course and I have often failed. But I do still try.

Become Your Own Hero

Many years would pass before I assimilated everything I had learnt from Glyn but, in the meantime, I had returned to university, been awarded a degree of sorts, joined NatWest Bank as a graduate entrant and briefly got married. My life was still troubled and unsettled but I seemed to be getting through the years adequately, if not yet with any measure of success.

It was during this period that I started to think about an event that had happened a few years previously, when I was in my late teens and growing up in South Wales. My friends and I had met some Welsh international rugby players in Cardiff (in Wales at the time rugby players were the equivalent of rock stars or better). My friends were in awe and they started bowing to them as if they were gods. I was shocked and embarrassed for my friends and, to be fair, the Welsh internationals seemed embarrassed too. The Welsh internationals were good rugby players but as people they were no better than any of us and did not deserve, or want, to be worshipped.

This gave me the idea of creating my own hero. Instead of worshipping false heroes like my foolish friends had done, I decided to take confidence in

---

the fact that as a person I was as good as anyone. I gradually developed that thought over several years by imagining what kind of person I would like to be in ten or twenty years' time. I slowly built up a portfolio of details about my future self, what qualities I would have, where I would live, what I thought and what I might achieve. Then I made that future self my hero and tried to live up to his ideals. More importantly I began to plan what I needed to do to become that person.

Eventually I succeeded. I imagined what kind of person I wanted to be by the date of my fortieth birthday. I planned what I had to do to get there and it worked. You can do it too.

... But Be Realistic

You have to set goals for yourself that are challenging but realistic. I finally set mine when I was thirty. The previous year I had left NatWest to join N M Rothschild, the investment bank, as a clerk in the lending department, and I decided that my hero (my future self) would become a director of Rothschild by the time he was forty. I thought that I possibly had the intellect to do it, although I truly wasn't certain about that. And I had no idea whether I had the necessary application to get there because, until then, I had not really applied myself to very much at all. So it was challenging in terms of my ability, but realistic in that I was already working for Rothschild, even though at that stage only as a clerk.

I also had an idea that at forty I would like to be married to someone I loved, maybe with a couple of children. I can't say this was a goal because I didn't realistically expect to achieve it. At the time I was still disentangling myself from my first short and unsuccessful attempt at marriage. So for this I didn't have a plan, although perhaps in matters of love it is better not to.

You might ask how I went about achieving my career goals. One way was by observation. I looked at how the most successful people in the bank dressed, how they looked, how they thought, how they spoke and how they behaved. And I copied them. Even today my suits are always plain, either dark blue or dark grey, and my work shirts are always white, because thirty-five years ago I decided to use one successful individual I worked with as a mentor. That individual subsequently went on to become a national figure and a member of the House of Lords so I suppose one rule that follows is to make sure you use the right mentor.

Had my goal been to become, say, an Olympic gold medallist, then obviously I would not have succeeded. Wishing and hoping is not enough, but if the goal is realistic and consistent with your abilities then hard work, long term planning and a measure of good luck can make it come true.

As it happened I had the great good fortune to meet and marry your Mum at the age of thirty-seven; Jack, the first born of our four children, arrived with ten months to spare before I turned forty; and I was appointed to the main Board of Rothschild two months after his birth.

I had become my own hero.

Embrace Failure

Never be afraid of, or embarrassed by, failures: be proud of them instead. A person who has never failed is a person who has never tried. Successful people don't avoid failing, they are successful because they don't give up. They try, fail and try again – and again. We learn from our failures, and without failing and understanding why we failed it is impossible ultimately to succeed.

Steve Jobs, the founder and CEO of Apple, got sacked from his own company in 1985 by the Chairman he had himself appointed only two years before. Jobs then was still only thirty years old. His next venture, a computer company appropriately called Next, consistently made losses. By the mid-1990s Apple itself was failing and looked impossible to save. Apple asked Jobs to come back as CEO, which he did in 1997. By the time he died in 2011 at the age of fifty-six, Apple was the largest and most profitable company in the world, and Jobs himself was described as the most outstanding and successful CEO in history.

My own story bears no resemblance to that of Steve Jobs, not least because he kept trying throughout his whole life, while for a long period I clearly didn't. From my mid-teens to my late twenties my life was a long list of almost continual failure including my academic achievements (poor), my career (a NatWest bank clerk with no obvious career moves) and my first marriage (enough said). I didn't begin to have any kind of success in my life until I was over thirty.

Without failures, usually many failures, success is not possible.

Put Your Hand Up

Say yes to opportunities whenever you can. Saying no just means another opportunity unexplored, another road not taken and closed off, usually forever.

When I was thirty-two I was asked if I would transfer from our London office to a new office in Hong Kong. The world was a much bigger place then and people were more parochial. Many would have turned down a move to Asia as being too risky and exotic, and fortunately one of my colleagues did just that. You see I was not the first choice for the posting, and the colleague who was asked before me decided he did not want to risk losing what he believed to be his safe career in London. So I was asked to go instead, agreed immediately, and less than three months later was on my way to live in Hong Kong, a city that would be my home for the next five years and where at first I knew not a single person.

The date of my departure was the pivot about which my life turned and from then on everything was transformed. Almost all I had done or achieved before that date had been mediocre or worse. Almost everything I touched afterwards seemed to be gilded with success. If my colleague had

---

not chosen to leave his own lifetime opportunity unexplored my life would have been very different and, amongst many other things, I would not have met your Mum and you would not have been born.

Be Decisive

In life, almost every important decision we have to make is based on insufficient evidence, by which I mean that the information available to us is never enough for us to be certain that our decision will be the right one. For some people the effect of this is permanent indecision, because they are afraid of being wrong.

In my experience, a decision that turns out to be wrong after properly considering all such information as is available is always better than no decision at all. A failure to make decisions, either in your personal life or in business, leads to a kind of paralysis where nothing is capable of being achieved. At least with a wrong decision you have an opportunity to rectify your mistake.

When I was asked to go to Hong Kong I decided to accept immediately. I had almost no information about what was involved and no rational basis to make any kind of decision. But I was by then trying to become my own hero, and I was not going to be able to do that as a thirty-two-year-old bank clerk in London.

Many people worry about being criticised for making wrong decisions. Here is a good quote:

'to avoid criticism say nothing, do nothing, be nothing'.

Seize the Moment

My decision to accept a posting to Hong Kong, shortly after it was suggested to me and without full information about what was involved, is an example of seizing the day. You may know the phrase from the Latin, which is 'carpe diem'. Yet a day is often too long to make decisions and sometimes it is necessary to act even more quickly.

I first became aware of the importance of time, and the uses of time, shortly after I joined Rothschild as a junior member of one of the teams. I reported to my team leader who in turn reported to a main Board director. The director would invite each of the teams (including the most junior members) to his office for a meeting once a week. In many respects this was similar to all other meetings I had attended: we made lists of what needed to be done; which clients were to be spoken to; what lawyers needed to be called, and so on. The difference was that, to the extent it was possible, the calls were made then, at that meeting, rather than, as had been my experience thus far, haphazardly over the forthcoming weeks whenever we had some spare time.

This did made the meetings longer, but I was surprised at how efficient a use of time it proved

---

and, most importantly, it was a great weapon against that great scourge of effective working: procrastination. It was there I learnt that, if something needs doing and it can be done now, do it now. Seize the moment.

The maxim has also proved true outside the office. I first met your Mum at supper in a friend's apartment in Hong Kong. She had recently arrived in the territory and knew very few people. I thought we got on well but I didn't see her again until about a week later. Perhaps a dozen of us were sitting around in a bar when, suddenly looking around, she asked if anyone played tennis. I thought that her gaze might have lingered a fraction longer on me than some of the others as she asked the question, but I could be mistaken. Anyway, my hand was up almost before she had finished talking.

Now I did not actually play tennis, at least not since childhood, and so I had to invest in new tennis gear and a new racket before our first game. I also arranged for that first game to take the form of a mixed doubles in order that my inadequacies in the sport could be better disguised. As it happened your Mum hadn't brought a racket with her either to Hong Kong and so I bought one for her as well.

You may think this was a heavy investment – two tennis rackets and a tennis outfit – but, as it turned out, no investment I have ever made ever generated such a handsome return.

If you think something is right for you, go for it. If it turns out you were mistaken you can always disentangle it later, but if you don't seize the opportunity when it is there you may lose it forever.

Be Curious

Successful people tend to be curious. They like to challenge accepted views and often become known for having views about most subjects that differ from the mainstream.

A curious person doesn't accept received wisdom, but wants to dig deeper to confirm whether or not the issue in question is true. A curious person asks questions, seeks flaws in arguments, challenges orthodoxies, and usually takes malicious delight in doing so as well. You will have noticed that I do this quite often, although you may not think it's my most attractive habit!

Most people when they are young believe something because someone once told them it was true. It is very rare for a child of Hindu parents to adopt Islam, or a child of Christian parents to embrace Judaism. Children generally follow the beliefs of their parents and their societies. Only when they become curious and start to think for themselves can such received views be challenged. Not all received wisdom is wrong, but little of it is ever wholly right. Not more than one of the faiths I have listed above can be wholly right as each of them conflicts with the others, but it is certainly possible that all of them could be wrong.

And it is not just in religion that this happens. In most areas of life, we are increasingly told things – through the media, in the workplace or by our peers – that are claimed to be 'true'. These assertions cover everything from dietary conventions to the fate of the planet. Some are true and some not. A few are not only untrue but irrational and damaging as well. The curious person wants to find out which is which.

In life never accept that anything should be done in a particular way because 'this is how we've always done it'. Never accept that anything is true because 'everybody knows' it to be. All human progress comes from doing and thinking differently and better.

A Bit About Shyness
and Embarrassment

From my early teens I was socially awkward, cripplingly shy and embarrassed about the smallest things. I also blushed at the slightest provocation, which was mortifying. Even at the age of twenty-eight, at a first meeting as the new assistant to a senior manager at NatWest, I was shaking so much from nerves he asked me if I was ill. It wasn't a good start.

Being unreasonably embarrassed about trivial things can affect the quality of our lives. It forces us to focus on the insignificant at the expense of what really matters. In my own early life who knows what opportunities I missed because I didn't have the courage, or was too embarrassed and shy, to pursue them. Only in later years did I start to make progress in achieving anything worthwhile.

Shy people have secrets that they don't want others to know because to tell would be the equivalent of giving a part of themselves away. They have secret fears too, of appearing stupid or ridiculous or being laughed at. They always find it difficult to believe or understand that other people wouldn't really care.

It is said that many people die at night in house fires because, in the smoke and confusion, they can't find their trousers; and by the time they do find them it's too late.

Always try to focus on the important rather than the trivial. Don't spend your life looking for your trousers when the house is burning down.

Managing Stress

Everyone suffers from stress. I suffered so acutely from it that I once told my dismayed father that my career ambition was to be a ticket collector on the London Underground (this was long before the introduction of automatic ticket barriers). I was serious too at the time. You turn up for work, collect tickets for eight hours and then go home – a completely stress-free day with no other responsibilities. Wonderful!

It was only gradually that I came to realise a fulfilled life requires much more than an absence of stress. In fact, a fulfilled life cannot be achieved entirely without stress, since a measure of stress is required to encourage the best from us. Problems only arise if stress levels rise beyond a point at which we can comfortably manage them, because too much stress can be a deadly blight on our ability to live fulfilled lives. We have to learn how to control it.

The first step towards taking control is to determine the reasons why we feel stressed. Here are some tips for the more common ones.

Perfectionism can be an important driver of success but it is also a major cause of stress. Don't set yourself up for failure by demanding that everything must be perfect all the time. Perfection is an absolute, but in real life we must learn that most times we have to live with 'good enough'. We all have too many things to deal with to be able to make any of them truly perfect.

Try not to worry about events that are outside your control. Once you have done what you can, there is nothing more to do. This also applies to other people, who, sadly, are also outside your control, at least most of the time. Because you can't control other people, don't get upset if they don't always do what you want. With events and with people, focus on what you can control when faced with a problem, rather than worrying about what you can't. And try not to get emotional – that never solves anything.

Manage your time as well as you can because poor time management always leads to stress. When you are struggling for time it is hard to stay calm and focused. If you plan ahead and stick to your schedule, however tempting it is not to, you can materially reduce your levels of stress (see also 'Don't be Late').

Break large tasks into smaller, more manageable units, and concentrate on completing each unit in turn. If you focus only on the unit you are completing, the larger picture will seem less daunting. Every large task is really only a series of small tasks, each one of which is relatively straightforward to complete as long as you have made them small enough.

Keep things in perspective. Ask yourself the questions: 'what is the worst thing that could happen if I don't complete this task?' and 'how important is my failure to do so going to seem next week, next month, next year?' Almost always the answers are 'not much' and 'not very' respectively. So why are you worrying? If the stress is affecting your ability to perform, go off and do something else for a while and come back to it later (see also 'We are Stardust').

When Bad Things Happen

Much of this book is about finding positives in our lives wherever they exist and minimising those setbacks that might seem important at the time but are really trivial in retrospect. These are simple life skills that enhance our lives.

In the course of a lifetime however everyone will experience bad things that are not trivial. These will involve grief and feelings of being unable to cope, perhaps of even feeling unable to go on. These are times when not only the heart buckles and stumbles into blackness, but the head, the stomach and the knees do too.

I have shared two such times with you, although you could not then have known the depth of my feeling. The first was when you were diagnosed with a malignant lymphoma at the age of nine and the second, after four months of intensive chemotherapy, when we learnt that – despite the treatment – a second tumour was growing inside you and you were not expected to survive. In those days a 'progression' of your particular lymphoma, which is the appearance of a second tumour after months of intensive chemotherapy, invariably led to death and we were told that you would be given the finest palliative care available during your last days.

I find that I cannot fully recall my thoughts during that terrible time. I can remember the effect on my mind though. It moved almost like a mechanical instrument, absorbed the new information, turned like the hands of a clock and clicked into its new position. I felt it almost in a physical sense. You were sick, that was now information that was known and suddenly acknowledged, and so, my mind asked, what were we going to do about it. Of course there was not necessarily anything we could do and, as I have said, specific thoughts are now lost to me, but I know my mind was set and ready for whatever was to come.

I don't know whether this is a common ability or not, but I seem to have been able – in life and in business – to deal with bad news by a rapid shift into thinking: this is the reality, what is the solution? Compared with coming so close to losing you the world of business seems relatively unimportant, but I have found even there that an ability to accept bad news quickly and take action immediately has salvaged deals that others had considered lost.

I know too that grief is part of life and that we will all suffer too much of it before we die. But I do believe that grief which goes on too long serves no purpose. On the contrary its effect is malign in that excessive grief hurts us as individuals as much or more than the original loss.

As it happened, while we were contemplating the prospect of palliative care for a matter of months at most while you gradually declined, your doctor came to me and said that he had heard reports of a boy in Germany with your condition who had lived, following a bone marrow transplant and an intensive programme of full body irradiation. He said that he was willing to try this procedure with you on two conditions. First that you were still physically strong enough to go ahead; and second that a perfect match for your bone marrow could be found amongst your siblings.

Although you were weak it was decided you were strong enough. The odds of finding a perfect match with a single sibling are only about one in four, but fortunately Rob, one of your three brothers, came up trumps and was able to provide the bone marrow you needed. There were still many months of painful radiotherapy to undergo and many dangers of infection that could have killed your weakened and unprotected body, but you survived.

And so most fortunately my thoughts on this particular issue of grief never came to be fully tested.

PART FOUR

ABOUT YOU AND OTHER PEOPLE

You Are Better Than No One...

... And no one is better than you. Many humans worry about their status in life and some are obsessed by it. You will be variously measured in your life by your wealth, education and knowledge, position in society, hereditary background, the way you speak and your use of certain social conventions, solely to determine where you are thought to stand in the social pecking order. It is all rather reminiscent of our hens in the top garden. People who are concerned about such things look down on those they perceive to be beneath them and look up to those they see as being above them. Some, who believe themselves to be at the lower end of the scale, look down on those above them too. George Bernard Shaw said: 'It is impossible for an Englishman to open his mouth without making some other Englishman hate or despise him'.

Things aren't now as bad as they were in Shaw's day, and they were already less so when I was your age. And the rules have changed too. When Shaw was writing in the early years of the twentieth century, the social pecking order was determined principally by one's position in society. Wealth, on its own, was considered rather vulgar if it was held in the form of anything other than landed estates. Wealth today perhaps carries more weight than position although, at least in the eyes of the majority, celebrity is now a serious challenger to both.

If you are sensible, you will treat the whole concept of status as something that might be appropriate for domestic poultry, but certainly not for humans. Always treat people with dignity whatever their status in life. Some of the less privileged have been unlucky, some feckless, some challenged by their genetic inheritance. Talk to them and treat them all as equals.

And make sure everyone else treats you on a comparable basis. It is possible that you will meet people in your life who think they are superior to you because their family is richer than yours or more famous, or they had a distant ancestor who was made a duke because his wife had become the king's mistress, or something similar. They aren't superior and the idea that they might be, for those reasons alone, is absurd.

You will meet others who have power over you, perhaps a future boss, and who like to show it. A boss who abuses power and talks down to you is never a good one, so grit your teeth as long as you can and if that doesn't work find another job.

Never think that anyone is better than you as a person. You may imagine that someone is cleverer, wittier, better looking or more athletic, but as a person you are just as good as they are.

I'm not saying that some people are not 'more good' than others, just that goodness does not depend on wealth, breeding, position in life, physical attributes or talents. It lies deeper than that.

What Do You Get When You Fall in Love?

Do you 'only get lies and pain and sorrow' as it says in the song? Well, sometimes you do but more often it's the best thing that can happen to you. The trouble is, at the start, you don't know which way it's going to go.

There is no doubt that falling in love can feel intoxicating, lifting you as high as you can get without chemical stimulation. A few years ago scientists tested a group of people who were all in the first stages of falling in love. They were each shown a photograph of their partner and the effect on their brains was monitored by an MRI scanner. The scans showed that the photographs stimulated the same part of the brain that is activated by the use of cocaine.

I know that on this subject, more than any other, you are unlikely to take advice from me and you certainly have the right not to, so I will restrict myself to two thoughts.

First, if it is to become a lasting relationship, you will need to accept the object of your affections as a whole and complete package, warts and all if he has them. Do not imagine that you are going to be able to improve his less good points over time. It won't happen, because people rarely change. In matters of love you have to accept your partner as he is, together with all his faults, or not accept him at all. It is true you may succeed in persuading him to hide his bad points for a while but they will inevitably re-emerge at a point in the relationship when you would doubtless prefer not to be reminded of them.

Second, love only really works when it is mutual and balanced. In your life, as in everyone's, you will love and be loved. Some will fall in love with you and you will fall in love with others. That is the nature of our lives. Treat those who love you gently if you don't love them too. And don't pursue anyone you love who doesn't feel the same about you. Such relationships don't work and will only leave you feeling miserable.

Above all don't chase love. It will come to you in its own good time.

On Friendship

Someone defined friends as people you like to be with at times when you don't actually have to be with them, but that understates their importance. Friends are not essential to the business of living but it is difficult to imagine a fulfilled life that does not include a few of them. The best of them will offer companionship, good counsel, mental stimulation and lots of laughter. Some of these attributes can be found elsewhere but only friends come with the full package.

Ultimately the only true way of having a friend is to be a friend, because friendship is something that is both received and given. It therefore requires on your part measures of generosity, loyalty, good humour and wisdom. Reciprocity is required in all relationships, whether with lovers, partners, friends or colleagues. If you don't give, you don't receive.

Most people of your age now keep in touch with their friends through social media, wherever they are in the world. In contrast all we had were landline telephones and letters through the post. As a result, I have lost touch with several of the closest friends I had from early in my life, which is one of my great regrets.

When I was a few years older than you, having recently married for the first time and about to move out of London with my new wife, I was worried about losing touch with the friends I had made there. And so, with three others, I agreed we would meet in London on the first Friday of every month for a drink. We hoped that with a system of monthly dues combined with fines for non-attendance, which together funded an annual October weekend away, we would be able to keep going for a few years at least, until growing families and other responsibilities intervened. Since then our little group has grown to a dozen, and more than forty years later we are still meeting. During all that time not a single monthly gathering has failed to take place.

I wouldn't recommend that you necessarily adopt such an extreme strategy to maintain your own friendships, but I do feel that something more than exchanging Facebook information on a regular basis is needed. Try to find ways of giving to good friends you rarely see as well as those you do.

Have Faith in People

Friends and others who are close to you will sometimes upset you by something they say or do. When this happens, don't automatically assume they have stopped liking you. Try to think of other possible explanations first.

You may have misunderstood what they said; or something bad or worrying may have happened to them; or perhaps they were just being tactless; or they may simply have been in a temporary bad mood themselves.

No one ever truly knows what other people are thinking, so you can never be sure why they seem to be acting in a particular way. If you always assume that when other people upset you it is because they don't like you, or they want to hurt or embarrass you, it diminishes your life beyond what has actually been said or done. If you assume that other people usually act with good intentions you may not always be right, but you will feel better about yourself.

Trusting people's good intentions doesn't always work, but trusting people is a better policy than not trusting them. If you do trust people, even people you don't know, most times you will be vindicated and the relationship you will have in the future with the person you have trusted will be immeasurably better. This is the case in business as well as in personal relationships. In the later years of my career, when many people were responsible to me, if I wanted someone to undertake a new assignment I would tell them in broad terms what it was I required them to do and then I would trust them to get on with it, subject to reporting back to me as each stage of the assignment was completed. Giving people responsibility through trust places a powerful obligation on them to deliver and they will try much harder not to let you down than if you simply give them detailed orders and stand over them while they do it.

In everyday matters I tend to trust most people I meet and I have rarely regretted doing so. On larger issues, particularly in business where the outcome is material, I try to evaluate the abilities and character of the person in whom I am intending to place my trust. This is because there is no point in trusting someone to complete a task that is beyond their capabilities and, if they fail for that reason, then it would be my evaluation that was flawed and my responsibility for the failure.

Occasionally someone will let you down. Tell them you are disappointed but otherwise let it go.

On the other hand, don't take this advice too far. Some people are genuinely unpleasant and undeserving of your trust. Learn how to identify such people and avoid them.

Be Tolerant

I know I don't need to tell you never to judge anyone on the basis of colour or gender, or any other personal characteristic. That seems such an uncontroversial and obvious statement now, but when I was your age I barely knew a single person who held such a view.

I was brought up at a time in Britain when racism and sexism were normal and where it was legal to refuse someone a job or accommodation because they were black, Irish, Jewish or female. When I was your age sex between consenting males was still a crime punishable by imprisonment; abortion was illegal even if the mother had been raped; and it was both legal and common practice to pay a woman less, and usually far less, than a man for doing an identical job.

Although we have come a long way as a society in just a few years, remember that tolerance is not something to be directed just towards people of different colours, genders and so on. You should show tolerance to everyone, because no person is without fault, no matter how hard we all try. If you have got to know yourself well enough to recognise your own faults and failings you will find it easier to tolerate and forgive the failings of others.

Although I am not religious I believe in religious tolerance and the right of individuals to practice the faith in which they believe, although this does not extend to a right of imposing their faith. Nobody has the right to say that they alone know the Truth if, in doing so, it involves the enforcement of that belief on others.

As for me, I do not know the Truth, whatever that word means. A general principle of mine, suggested to me by a former boss (and another mentor) early in my career, is 'never to believe in anything one hundred per cent'. It is a principle that, during my life, has protected me from all kinds of plausible rogues: social, commercial and political rogues as well as religious.

Families Are People Too

Don't judge family members by standards that are different from those you apply to other people. They will all have some of the attributes as well as many of the failings of everyone else in this world. An important part of becoming an adult, a rite of passage if you will, is learning to accept that parents and other members of the family are people too.

Parents can also expect too much of their children. During the years I was Chairman at Terra Nova School I rarely met a parent who didn't think their son or daughter was perfect, even though some of their children seemed to have no concept of acceptable behaviour or any apparent desire to be educated.

When I was younger, that would also have been a good description of me. I don't think your mother was an angel either.

The point is that we are all stuck into this together: into our families, into our communities, into our countries and into our world. We all just have to try to pull together to make it work. We can't individually do much about our world, or even our country, but we can help to make our families

---

and our communities work. We all have the power
to do that if we also have the will.

Make Other People Happy

One of the ways we get to feel good in life is by making other people happy. That's curious, because it's not immediately obvious why our efforts to benefit others would have anything to do with our own welfare. It works because we are genetically programmed to respond positively to our own good works, and being altruistic therefore has the effect of making us feel good. Scientists have struggled to explain why this should be from the viewpoint of evolutionary biology, but they do not dispute that the effect exists.

One of the easy ways to make other people happy is to give them presents. I don't mean the kind of presents that are tied up in wrapping paper and distributed on birthdays and Christmas. In life the best presents you can give to others are a compliment, a funny comment, an offer of help, a word of encouragement, or even a friendly smile. If you give gifts like these to everyone you meet you will be astonished at the effect it has, not just on the people you give them to, but on you as well.

The opposite is also true. Mean words, cross looks and short tempers not only reinforce your own bad mood but also have a depressing effect on everyone around you.

Don't Be Late

Every minute someone is late for an appointment means a minute wasted for someone else. If it is a meeting where more than two people are involved, then many people will be wasting their time. Being late is telling other people that your time is more important than theirs. Friends may forgive you but they won't be amused by it and they will probably think a little less of you. I'm sure you don't like it either when you are waiting for someone else who is late for an appointment with you.

Being late also has run-on consequences. If you are late for a hair appointment your hairdresser may find that she too, still working on your hair, is late for her next customer and so that person is kept waiting as well.

Most of the time being late is just irritating to other people, but as your life develops it will become a more important issue. There will be times when you will be meeting people, in your personal life as well as business, who will not readily identify with the fact that you think your time is more important than theirs. Then it will start to affect your career and your life.

Give everyone you meet the gift of punctuality.

Do the Right Thing

This sounds like a moral instruction of the sort that I have promised not to make. It isn't. Rather, it is a tool for reaching the best decision when facing a moral dilemma of the type that we sometimes encounter in life. By this I mean a situation where we have to make a decision at work, in family life or elsewhere, and where all of the choices open to us will cause some hurt to someone, often someone we like or love and who perhaps doesn't deserve to be hurt. These are the hardest of all decisions to make.

We do the right thing by first removing ourselves and our personal interests from all consideration. Then we ask ourselves what the right thing to do is. This sounds trite but it does work. I said earlier that people generally have an innate sense of what is right and wrong, and what is fair and what is not. This is the time to use that innate sense. You will find that it simplifies the decision-making process and leads you quickly to a decision.

In my life I have often found myself floundering and wondering what to do about a problem that needed to be resolved. Only when I started to consider what was the right thing to do did the solution become apparent. I have also found that the process of reaching the decision in turn provides the strength to implement it, which is itself often a difficult and unpleasant task.

PART FIVE

BEING HUMAN

Danger and Fear

Danger is real, but fear is only in our minds. Don't confuse the two. Fear is an evolutionary mechanism that warns us of potential dangers, but sometimes our wires get crossed and we become afraid when there is no real danger at all. When this happens our ability to live fulfilled lives is compromised.

Our big brains began to evolve on the African savannas hundreds of thousands of years ago when our ancestors lived in small groups as hunter-gatherers. Their dangers were real and all around them and I'm sure their days were full of fear. In those days, one in two of all human deaths was violent and probably up to half of those was a result of violence by another human. Those African savanna people thought that almost everything was a threat, and they were right. Because our brains have not evolved much since then many people today think this is still the case, but they are wrong.

Although our ancestors were clever they were unable to think in big numbers and our own brains still have difficulty in thinking in numbers much larger than the number of people in one of those ancient tribes. That is why we are so bad

---

at understanding the probability of rare events happening. Our African savanna brains are fooled into thinking that if something can happen then more than likely it will happen. In Africa all those years ago it would have been true. Today it isn't.

A Bit About Probability

Here is an example. Some people worry about being murdered if they are out on the streets of a big city late at night. The probability of being murdered in a single lifetime in Britain is one in 85,000. Perhaps that doesn't sound too comforting to our ancient brains but think of it this way. The equivalent of 85,000 days is 232 years. If we go backwards in time for 232 years it is the year 1784. Now the game I want you to play is that I think of a single random date (day, month and year) between 1784 and 2016 and then ask you to guess what it is. You have only one guess. What do you think the probability is of you being right? Pretty close to zero I'd say – it would seem to be a miracle if you did guess it! Actually, it is exactly the same as the probability of being murdered.

You can do this with all kinds of facts by changing the probability into days and years. The probability of being killed by a shark if you are swimming in the sea is about one in 10 million. This is such an enormous number that, in terms of days, we have to go back to beyond 25,000 BC before we can play our guessing the date game. That means guessing correctly a single day in more than 27,000 years. You are not going to do it. Also you are not going to be killed by a shark.

Now work out the equivalent number of years that corresponds to the odds of being killed in a plane crash (one in 4.7 million). It's a very long time.

Never let fears about something with a vanishingly small probability stop you from climbing the mountain.

Make Reason Your Guide

Changing probabilities into days and years to make them less scary is an example of using reason, or logic, to counter irrational fears and superstitions. The ability to think logically has modified our African savanna brains and enabled us to create, against all odds, a civilisation incomparably safer than our African savanna past.

It is true that large parts of the world remain in conditions of relative superstition and savagery, and it is also true that other parts sometimes revert back into such conditions. Sometimes the savagery can seem so awful that many people fear the world may be regressing into a dark age rather than the reverse. But that would be to take too short term a view. Little more than 400 years ago men were being burnt at the stake in Britain for holding mildly divergent religious beliefs. Though terrible events continue to occur with depressing frequency, the long-term trend towards enlightenment during the last five centuries, not just in Britain but throughout many parts of the world, is undeniable, and thrillingly clear.

For those who argue that life used to be so much better in the old days, and there are many who do, remind them about antiseptics, antibiotics and anaesthesia and ask them to imagine what life would have been like without them. It meant death through any random infection and operations conducted with a rag in your mouth to stifle your screams. And that just relates to progress from three recent scientific advances that begin with the letter 'A'.

Reason is what has made such progress possible. Reason provides the pillars that support our society. It gives us laws and justice that can no longer be arbitrarily applied by tyrants as long as we are vigilant. It gives us the scientific method, which has created great industries from which all the material goods that we now take for granted have poured. It can explain the origins of our world and our place within it. And ultimately it is only reason that will be able to protect our future and our planet.

Most importantly reason helps to eliminate fear, and freedom from fear is the greatest freedom of all.

The Creative Arts

No human society has existed in which music, dancing and painting have not formed some part. The earliest Spanish cave paintings date back 40,000 years, a time that corresponds with the first known appearance of Homo Sapiens in Europe, while music and dancing have been part of celebrations, religious ceremonies and simple entertainment ever since. Ornaments too have been found in every society, wrought from gold, bronze and precious jewels and of great intricacy and beauty.

It seems that humans have an underlying affinity with the creative arts – not necessarily to create anything worthwhile themselves because only a small number have the ability to do so – but rather to experience that which has been created.

In the Western world in the last 500 years, there has been enormous growth in the depth, complexity and variety of creative arts, by which I mean painting, sculpture, music in all its forms, literature, poetry, cinema and all the rest. They all seem to be able to provide an experience to humans that transcends our normal lives and thereby enriches them. I don't think complexity is necessary, or even desirable if it makes an artwork inaccessible to us. But quality is essential. I'm not going to try to explain what I mean by quality here, which is a very slippery concept, but as humans we seem to be able to learn to recognise it when it is present even if we can't precisely define what it is. Sometimes the recognition takes a little effort but the effort is always worthwhile.

I don't differentiate between so-called high art and low art. There is quality present in Abba and Adele, in Beethoven and the Beatles, in Shakespeare and Shaw, in Picasso, Michelangelo and Banksy. And so on. When listening to music, or reading a poem, or looking at a painting, ask the question: 'where is the quality?' It may be the melody or the harmonies; or the way the flowing words of a poem evoke a person or a landscape; or in the colours or the brushwork of a painting; or in none or all of these things. When you discover where the quality is you will enjoy the creation all the more.

I believe that experiencing art, in its widest sense, is so fundamental to our being human that it is a necessary part of living a fulfilled life. You already know literature and I'm sure you will have found some writing that you love. If you look beyond literature to some of the other creative arts, you will find whole new worlds to explore.

... And Crafts

The human urge to create, and the ability to appreciate quality in that which has been created, is everywhere. Anyone who has looked with approval upon a garden, or a fine piece of furniture, or a building or a painting has felt it. A sense of satisfaction and rightness about what has been created is fundamental to us all.

And even though few can aspire to the creation of true art, we can all participate in bringing quality into our lives in lesser forms. It can be as simple as a well-decorated room or the creation of a delicious meal or a particularly fine arrangement of flowers. All who bring quality to their lives, whether as chefs, florists, actors, plumbers, musicians, basket weavers or even (some) bankers, enhance their own lives as well as those of others.

And get a hobby, even though that is a word more associated with elderly people tending allotments or collecting stamps, which are actually fine as hobbies although perhaps not for you just now. Anyway, whether you call them hobbies or interests they are just a way of participating in crafts, that lesser branch of the creative arts to which we can ourselves contribute.

Interests outside our normal daily existence are essential to a fulfilled life. As humans, for whatever reason, we aspire to a higher level than that required for the bare means of living and we struggle, unfulfilled, if we fail to achieve it.

Seek out quality in all that you do, within you as well as in the world around you.

Sports and Games

Humans, like all animals, have an evolutionary urge to be competitive. It was competition that led to the evolution of our big brains, a development that eventually enabled us to win the battle of survival on the African savanna. Sports and other games allow us to satisfy that competitive urge in a 'safe' environment where the result ultimately doesn't matter. I know some football fans will disagree strongly with that statement and that people who take playing sport seriously will too, but however much we seem to care about who wins a sporting event, they are wrong. Sport is not life, just a part of it.

Sports and games are played in artificial environments like a stadium, a court or a games table that represent stylised forms of the real world. In that stylised world you can learn much: how to develop a determination to win; how tactics and strategy can improve the possibility of winning; how to win and lose with grace; how to respect an opponent. These are skills you will need in real life, and sports and games give an opportunity for you to develop them without adverse consequences if, at first, you get things wrong.

Participation in these activities satisfies our evolutionary need for competition and, rather in the same way as the creative arts, removes us for a time from the pressures of living. Even for spectators a sporting event can be as intense and involving as it is for those participating, although obviously without the exercise.

In the course of a lifetime an individual will suffer many triumphs and disasters, all of which can be difficult to manage. In the real world how one deals with such events is critical. People who have an inability to cope with losing often stop participating, which is as true in sport as it is in life.

Don't stop participating! Get some practice in first if you can, on the tennis court, the netball court or the hockey pitch.

Be a Good Citizen

Develop your own views on important issues: global, national and local. Don't expect to leave all decisions to others and then hope that the decisions will be benign. Try to understand the issues, which will involve reading, thought and consideration. It may be a chore – though it really shouldn't be – but more importantly it's a duty. If you don't do it who will?

In Britain we have a democracy that is not in good shape because the majority of people don't care enough, and paradoxically they don't care because democracy has been remarkably successful in producing, on the whole, a fair and tolerant society. It may not seem like that to many of those who have little, but go back a century or two and those same people would have been facing destitution, starvation, debtor's prison or the workhouse. Life really has got better for everyone, not only in this country but also in many other countries throughout the world. This does not mean we should be complacent – far from it – because further improvements need to be made and also because this isn't necessarily a natural state (see 'Be Tolerant' for what it used to be like); our democracy needs to be supported and respected if it is to survive. The concept that 'all that is necessary for evil to triumph is for good people to do nothing' is well known. We have seen it happen throughout history.

Most days, somewhere in the world, somebody dies protesting for the right to have 'a government of the people, by the people, for the people' in that majestic phrase from the field of Gettysburg. In Britain many people have died over hundreds of years for the same cause. Magna Carta happened 800 years ago, the Great Reform Bill was passed 184 years ago and it was only 88 years ago that all adult citizens were given the right to vote – a year when my mother and father were alive. Full adult suffrage is so fundamental and yet, even in Britain, it happened so recently.

As a woman, you have a particular debt to the suffragettes who protested and fought and suffered in order that you could be added to the franchise and be allowed to participate in decisions that affect us as a nation.

When I was younger, and lived in a more imperfect society, I went on many mass demonstrations to protest about some injustice or other. I was often asked: 'What is the point? It won't make any difference.' My rather pompous answer was always the same. 'The difference I make by being there is small, but it is finite.'

It's the same with my vote. And yours.

Sex ...

No book called 'How to Live' can avoid the subject of sex. However, I have promised no moral sermons and so I will confine myself to two observations based on experience.

Sex with someone you don't know or don't much like is rarely satisfactory.

Sex with someone you love, and who loves you in turn, is usually great and sometimes transcendental.

Everything in between is your call.

... And Drugs ...

Most illegal drugs, in their purest forms, are a lot less dangerous than governments and the media would have us believe. The biggest dangers are from toxic impurities contained within them or by users underestimating their strength. So called 'legal highs' are also dangerous for similar reasons.

Legalising and licensing drugs would reduce these dangers, remove the connection with criminal gangs and lead to fewer deaths. Colorado and other States have already legalised cannabis and I expect this trend will continue. Most drugs will probably become legal in most countries in your lifetime and will thereby become controlled for strength, purity and distribution in the same way that alcohol is now.

For the time being both illegal drugs and legal highs are a bit of a lottery and best avoided. If you do take them make it as rare an event as you can and keep the amounts small. Many drugs offer a 'high' in exchange for dependency, but do try to avoid heroin and nicotine. The former will make you so dependent that it will kill you quickly. Nicotine, unique amongst all drugs as far as I am aware, offers only a strong dependency but without providing any 'highs' at all. Instead

---

it gives you 'lows' that can only be cured by more nicotine. It is therefore quite the most pointless drug invented. I speak as a former addict.

... And Rock & Roll

The best Rock & Roll is always great.

About Alcohol

As an enthusiastic and regular consumer of alcohol myself, I am ill-qualified to give you dispassionate advice on this subject. In fact, as you have pointed out to me on several occasions, I drink more than is generally recommended by even the most liberal of medical authorities. Your brother Rob, when he was very young, was asked to write an essay at school on 'My Father'. The entire essay consisted of the following: 'He likes to drink beer and fall asleep on the sofa.' While there may have been some truth in this, it was not best designed to impress the school authorities as to my fitness as a parent, let alone a future Chairman of Governors.

First, let us be clear: alcohol is a dangerous drug and one that would itself be illegal if the laws that prohibit the sale of illegal drugs were applied consistently. More than 8,000 people die in Britain from alcohol-related conditions each year while hospital admissions related to alcohol consumption have recently topped one million annually. Medical conditions relating to alcohol and leading to death include cirrhosis of the liver and cancers of the throat, breast, stomach, liver and bowel.

This is a grim litany that leads to the question:

why would anyone want to drink at all? One answer is that drinks containing alcohol come in a huge variety of flavours, none of which taste like anything else available, and many of which most people find delicious. A second is its role as a social lubricant that facilitates relationships with others. A third, to which I have already alluded, is that humans are not simply machines for living but constantly require to be stimulated in ways that have nothing to do with mere existence. The consumption of alcohol, and other drugs, for this reason has a bizarre connection with an appreciation of the creative arts.

I must be careful not to say that any of this justifies, or makes acceptable, the indiscriminate drinking of alcohol. Here are some reasons why becoming a regular or a binge drinker is not OK: you may be seriously embarrassed and shamed by what you have unknowingly got up to while drunk; you will be more at risk of physical violence and non-consensual sex; drunkenness and its close relative, the hangover, will make managing the other parts of your life and career much more difficult; and there is a good chance that you will die younger than you otherwise would have done.

When you do choose to drink, make sure that you are always in control. The people I have known who succumbed to drink and are now dead were those who drank aggressively in short periods and regularly lost control. You always knew them at parties and social gatherings by their behaviour: loud and sometimes offensive early on and comatose later.

What a Wonderful World

The lyrics of the song of this name, made famous by the great old jazz trumpeter and singer, Louis Armstrong, are mawkishly sentimental but the concept is true: the world is an amazing place.

The natural world contains so much beauty that no single person can reasonably hope to see it all. Just exploring everything that is worth seeing in mainland Britain can take up most of a lifetime. If you add to that the world's great mountain ranges, rivers, forests and deserts the task can begin to seem too daunting. Don't let that put you off though – the sooner you start the better.

I do sometimes wonder why the natural world we live in seems to humans to be so beautiful. For those who believe in a supreme being the answer is obvious: the world was made for us. For people like me who reject that concept the answer is more difficult. It is possible that the very notion of what we understand by beauty has been hardwired into us by our perception of the natural world; in other words, we perceive to be beautiful that which exists.

An alternative explanation is that certain conditions must apply to any planet capable of producing life, or at least the life we are familiar with on the world we currently occupy. There must be an atmosphere that contains oxygen; and water must exist in sufficient abundance, and in a form, that makes it readily available to living organisms. Such a planet must almost certainly contain a liquid core, some of which being able to escape from time to time through volcanoes or through deep undersea vents, bringing heat and new chemicals to the mix on the surface. Some think that life itself began beneath oceans around volcanic vents that produced the warmth and the chemicals that were to spark into primitive organisms.

Whatever the truth about the origins of life, the key constituents – an atmosphere, abundant water and a liquid core – have shaped our world. Its surface is divided into zones, which we call tectonic plates, and which move independently across the liquid core, colliding with other plates and squeezing the land between into serrated mountains. The Himalayas began to be formed millions of years ago when the Indian plate collided with the Eurasian plate and this process is still continuing. Meanwhile, erosion caused by water in the form of oceans, rain and rivers, together with a mobile atmosphere – which you and I know as wind – grinds down over millennia everything that is being built up. The result is a world of infinite diversity and breath-taking beauty; and it is populated by a myriad of life forms, each one of which merits a lifetime of study.

Humans too have contributed immensely to the diversity of the planet. Although what they create isn't always beautiful, some of it is magnificent. All of the great cities of the world are capable of inspiring awe and we have one of them very close – London. Elsewhere there are cities and cultures and people that will enthral you. I was lucky enough to live for five years in Hong Kong and, as I have said, it was an experience that changed my life.

The world is waiting – get out and immerse yourself in its wonders!

We Are Stardust

The biggest intellectual shock I've ever had was when I discovered that every atom of which I am composed was once part of the centre of a star now long vanished. After 'Big Bang', 13.7 billion years ago, the hydrogen and helium that it created coalesced over countless ages to form stars. These two elements were then transformed through nuclear fusion – which is what creates the heat and light of stars – into all the other elements that now exist, including the carbon, nitrogen and oxygen of which, together with hydrogen, we are mostly made. Occasionally one of these stars exploded, blasting the new elements across the galaxy in a blaze of light. We call exploding stars 'supernovae' and they are so rare that the last star to explode in our galaxy – the Milky Way – was seen on Earth more than 400 years ago.

But this was only the start. Over billions of years, millions of stars exploded in this way, creating new elements that drifted across the galaxy until they were attracted by gravity to new stars, one of which was our Sun. Then the elements began to coalesce into planets until, about 4.5 billion years ago, the Earth on which we live was formed. Afterwards life began to develop and evolve and over a further unimaginable period of time you and I came to exist.

It all reminds me of Douglas Adams's Total Perspective Vortex in *The Hitchhikers Guide to the Galaxy*, a wise and funny book that you should read. When you are put into the Vortex you are given just one momentary glimpse of the entire unimaginable vastness of the universe and all that is in it, and somewhere there is a tiny mark, a microscopic dot, which says, 'You are here'. In the book, the knowledge that people thereby gained of their own insignificance destroyed the minds of almost everyone who experienced it.

For me, learning that we are all made from the dust of vanished stars was the equivalent of being placed into the Total Perspective Vortex, although it didn't destroy my mind at all. On the contrary, it made all the little worries and fears that trouble us seem triflingly small.

What a Piece of Work is Man (and Woman Too)

Our situation is truly terrifying. We exist on a small ball of rock, whirling around an unimportant star through a vacuum, protected only by a small covering of atmosphere that, for anywhere more than five miles above the surface, is unable to sustain us. Our own star, the Sun, is one of 100 billion stars in our galaxy and our galaxy is one of more than 100 billion other galaxies. These are numbers so large that even the use of reason can't make sense of them, but amongst all that immensity Earth is still the only place we know for sure that is capable of sustaining human life.

And yet evolution, from this least promising of circumstances, using a combination of blind genetic chance and the ruthless destruction of any organism unable to compete effectively for scarce resources, has developed a creature that is self-aware and able to understand how it came to be. How extraordinary is that!

From subsisting as Palaeolithic hunter-gatherers humans have created a civilisation in little more than 10,000 years – the equivalent of a single heartbeat in comparison with the age of the universe. Not a perfect civilisation it is true, but one that contains the notions of laws and justice, science, art, sculpture and music; and which can predict and experimentally confirm the origins of the universe to within the smallest fraction of a second following Big Bang.

Physically, humans are almost certainly unique in the entire vast universe; the blind chance results of evolution over billions of years would never succeed in creating the same creature twice. Of course, if other intelligent creatures do exist, there may be similarities in form, but that is all.

Humans may also be unique in possessing intelligence, self-awareness and creative brilliance. We don't know, and we don't yet have enough information to calculate, the probability of creatures with such talents emerging elsewhere, but it is certainly possible we are the only ones.

So be proud, not only because you are a unique being yourself, but also because you are a member of a unique and remarkable species.

And Finally

Do you remember a story I once told you about a girl who cried and cried because she had no shoes, until she met another girl who had no feet?

Don't live in sadness and disappointment regretting what you haven't got. Focus instead on what you have. Celebrate the joys of living rather than waste your life cursing the frustrations.

Try this: towards the end of each day choose at least one good thing that happened that day however small and insignificant it might seem and reflect on it. Then think how grateful you should be for having experienced that special day – a day that like all days, once gone, will never come again.

And what could be more special than that?